A Hunt for Clues

Written by Anne Miranda • Illustrated by Michele Noiset

"Oh, no," said Mary Sue.
"Puff is gone."

"Please help me find my cat, Puff."

"We will help," said Burt.
"True Blue can hunt for clues.
True Blue can find Puff."

True Blue found a clue on the curb.

"That is Puff's tag," said Mary Sue.

"Good dog," said Burt. "I told you
True Blue could hunt for clues."

True Blue found a clue in the mud.

"That is Puff's toy," said Mary Sue.

"Good dog," said Burt. "I told you
True Blue could hunt for clues."

True Blue found a clue in the house.

"That is Puff's ball," said Mary Sue.

"Good dog," said Burt. "I told you
True Blue could hunt for clues."

Mary Sue heard a purr.

There was Puff, sleeping in a box.

"True Blue did it.
He found Puff," said Burt.

"Yes," said Mary Sue.

"Maybe True Blue CAN hunt for clues."

"But what True Blue can
really do best is eat."